Read-About® Health

Allergies

By Sharon Gordon

Consultants
Nanci R. Vargus, Ed.D.
Assistant Professor
Literacy Education
University of Indianapolis
Indianapolis, Indiana

Jayne L. Waddell, R.N., M.A., L.P.C.
School Nurse/Health Educator/Lic. Professional Counselor

Children's Press®
A Division of Scholastic Inc.
New York   Toronto   London   Auckland   Sydney
Mexico City   New Delhi   Hong Kong
Danbury, Connecticut

Designer: Herman Adler Design
Photo Researcher: Caroline Anderson
The photo on the cover shows a girl with an allergy to pollen.

Library of Congress Cataloging-in-Publication Data

Gordon, Sharon.
  Allergies / by Sharon Gordon.
    p. cm. — (Rookie read-about health)
Includes index.
Summary: Simple text describes allergies, their effects, and discusses
some of the most common allergens.
  ISBN 0-516-22581-2 (lib. bdg.)   0-516-27394-9 (pbk.)
  1. Allergy in children—Juvenile literature. [1. Allergy.] I. Title.
II. Series.
  RJ386 .G674 2003
  616.97—dc21
                                        2002015123

CHILDREN'S PRESS, AND ROOKIE READ-ABOUT®,
and associated logos are trademarks and or registered trademarks
of Grolier Publishing Co., Inc. SCHOLASTIC and associated logos
are trademarks and or registered trademarks of Scholastic Inc.

1 2 3 4 5 6 7 8 9 10 R 12 11 10 09 08 07 06 05 04 03

Achoo!

What made you sneeze?
Is it the cat?

You might have an
allergy (AL-er-jee)!

5

6

That means your body may change when you are near a cat.

It might feel like you have a bad cold.

Your nose might run.
Your eyes might water
or get puffy. You might
start sneezing—a lot!

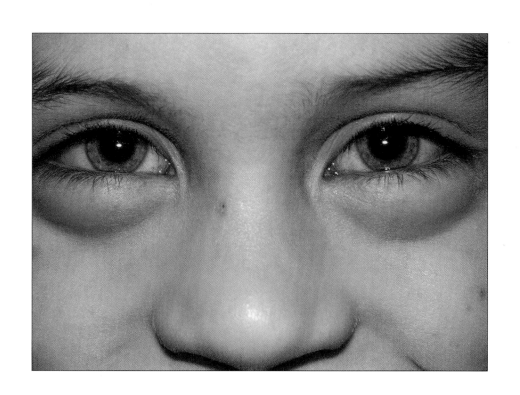

9

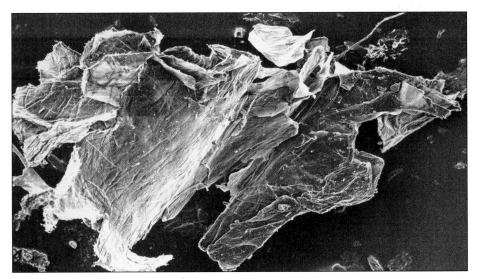

Close-up of a piece of dust

10

One out of five people have allergies.

There may be something they should not breathe in, touch, or taste.

If they do, they will have an *allergic reaction* (uh-LER-jik ree-ACK-shun).

Some people have food allergies. They cannot eat certain foods, such as milk, eggs, peanuts, or shellfish.

If they eat these foods, they may get red, itchy bumps called *hives*.

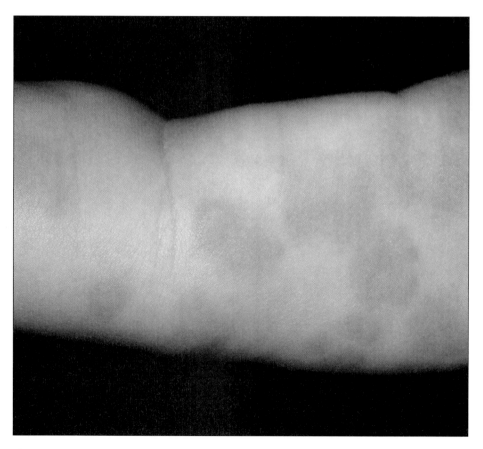

Their throats may start to
feel tight. They may have
trouble breathing.

Did you ever get stung by a bee?

It always hurts.

People with allergies to bee stings are in real danger!

17

The sting might swell up a lot. People might have a hard time breathing.

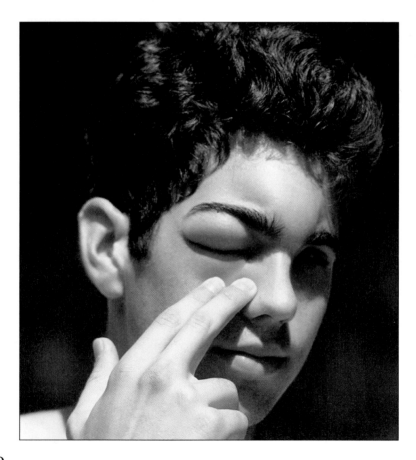

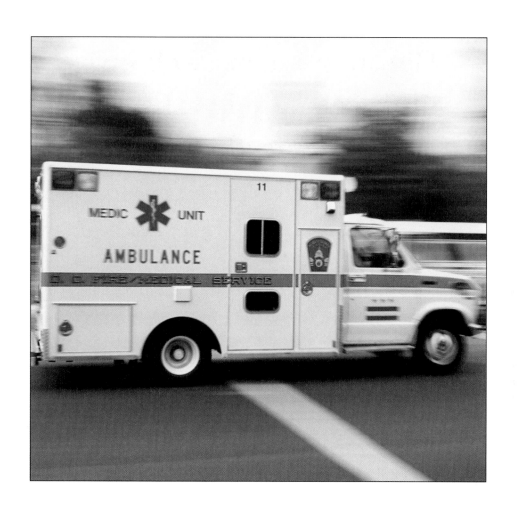

They need to get help
right away!

pollen

Springtime is a beautiful season. It is not always fun for some people with allergies.

Flowers give off *pollen*. Pollen helps plants spread their seeds.

Many people have allergies to pollen.

Some people with springtime allergies need to stay indoors or take medication (med-ih-CAY-shun).

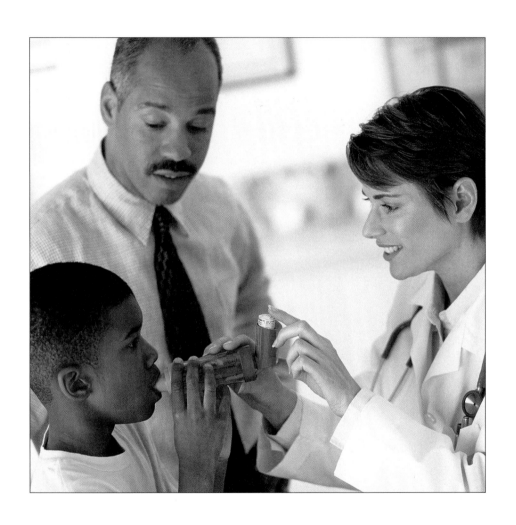

24

Having an allergy changes the way you live.

You must stay away from certain things.

You need to know what to do for help.

The good news is that you may outgrow some of your allergies.

The bad news is that you can also get new ones.

Achoo!

Words You Know

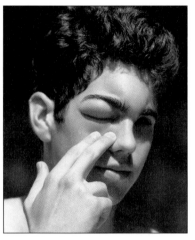

allergic reaction

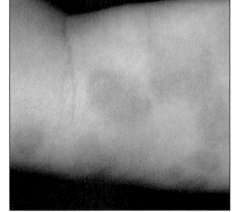

allergy

flowers

hives

30

Index

About the Author

Sharon Gordon is a writer living in Midland Park, New Jersey. She and her husband have three school-aged children and a spoiled pooch. Together they enjoy visiting the Outer Banks of North Carolina as often as possible.

Photo Credits

Photographs © 2003: Corbis Images/Michael Keller: 24, 31 top right; Custom Medical Stock Photo: cover, 6; Photo Researchers, NY: 13 top left (Phillip Hayson), 20 (Damien Lovegrove/SPL), 9, 14, 30 bottom right (Dr. P. Marazzi/SPL), 10 top left, 30 bottom left (Gary Meszaros); PhotoEdit: 3, 29, 31 bottom right (Mary Kate Denny), 23, 31 top left (Myrleen Ferguson Cate), 27 (Tony Freeman), 18, 30 top left (Robert W.Ginn), 5, 30 top right (Michael Newman), 26 (Mark Richards), 13 top right, 15, 20 bottom right, 31 bottom left (David Young-Wolff); The Image Works: 13 bottom right (Bill Bachmann), 10 top right (Sean Cayton), 17 (Townsend P. Dickinson), 19 (Mark Reinstein), 13 bottom left (Joe Sohm); Visuals Unlimited/Gary Gaugler: 10 bottom.

indoors

medication

pollen

sneeze

31